HANDBOOKS OF EUROPEAN NATIONAL DANCES

EDITED BY
VIOLET ALFORD

※※-※※

DANCES OF SPAIN

II : North-East and East

Plate 1   Valencia

DANCES of SPAIN

II: North-East and East

LUCILE ARMSTRONG

NOVERRE PRESS

ILLUSTRATED BY
LUCILE ARMSTRONG
ASSISTANT EDITOR
YVONNE MOYSE

First published in 1950
This edition published in 2021 by
The Noverre Press
Southwold House
Isington Road
Binsted
Hampshire
GU34 4PH

ISBN 978-1-914311-14-7

CONTENTS

᳁᳁᳁᳁᳁

Illustrations in Colour, pages 2, 12, 29, 39
Map of Eastern Spain, page 6

EASTERN SPAIN

BASQUE
PROVINCES

FRANCE

NAVARRE

Anso

Hecho

Jaca   Ainsa

Andorra

OLD CASTILE

Huesca

CATALONIA   Rosas

Manlléu

Ebro

Castelltersol

Saragossa

Caldas de Montbuy

Mollet

ARAGON

San Estéve de
Sasrovires

Barcelona

NEW CASTILE

VALENCIA

Valencia

Alcoy

BALEARIC ISLANDS

MURCIA

N
W   E
S

MEDITERRANEAN SEA

INTRODUCTION

THE first Handbook on Dances of Spain gave a short survey of the art in Andalusia, the Central tableland and the North-West provinces.* If Andalusia means Spain to us, as it does to far too many people, then in a Catalan village looking on to the Mediterranean we shall find it hard to believe we are in Spain at all. As for the villages of Alto Aragón cowering amongst the snow and rock of the Pyrenees, there we shall disbelieve it altogether—until the dances begin.

The vast province of Aragón, reaching from the high Pyrenees to the borders of Valencia, contains the Alacay (a Basque-influenced Chain dance of the Anso and Hecho valleys) and passes through the zone of the nimble Jota to dances in the graceful Valencian style.

The Aragonese passionately claim the Jota as their possession, but in reality it is known nearly all over the Peninsula. It is said to be derived from the Andalusian Fandango and to have been brought by an exiled Moorish poet, Aben Jot, to the north. The dance today consists of at least forty steps, some of which are selected by the man, the woman following. Jota rhythm is 3/4; the dance begins always with the step described on page 33, going on to any others desired, strung together by the Estribillo. The Jota singer lifts up his strident voice and sings a verse during the Estribillo, while the dancers may rest. Its chief characteristic

* The Basque provinces will be dealt with in the forthcoming Pyrenean Handbook: *Dances of France*, vol. III.

is an almost cat-like agility attained by much-flexed knees, immediately straightened again. There are other dances in Aragon, needless to say, but when the province is mentioned every Spaniard I have ever met preens himself and remarks, 'Ah! La Jota'. It is not now a true folk dance. Music and topical Coplas are constantly being composed; many of these last suggestive, amusing or tragic. The dance has many variants and one hardly ever sees it performed twice in the same way.

⚜ CATALONIA ⚜

This mountain and coastal province derives much of its culture from Provence and Languedoc. French Roussillon is Catalan also, but cut off by mountains and politics from its sister country in Spain.

Nothing could be richer than the Catalan treasury of dance, comprising from five to six hundred folk dances. Their chief characteristic is a finish and delicacy unknown elsewhere—at least in Europe. In Northern Catalonia dances and style are typically Pyrenean: strong leaps for the men, downcast eyes and low steps for the women. In the mountains dances are fairly simple, often with small figures, cutting their coat to suit the cloth, in the confined spaces of some rocky village. It is not until we come to the richer villages of the foothills that we see the Sardana—Catalonia's real national dance.

The Sardana. This much-written-of dance (and a great deal of nonsense has been written too) is not of any great age. It must have sprung from one of the many Chain dances, which became a Round. It was probably put into its present shape by a village musician, Pep Ventura—but not, as is constantly said, invented by him. It takes more than one man to make a folk dance. Men and women stand alternately holding hands and facing inwards. There are two steps, the Curts (shorts) and the Llargs (longs), always

8

beginning with the left foot and moving slightly to the left, then slightly to the right. A leader who is soon projected from each ring of dancers takes command, counting the bars and signalling the changes. To these bare bones intricate steps are added by the men.

The Contrapás. A much older form of dance is the Contrapás, a Chain shaped into a wide segment of a circle. It used to be a ceremonial dance of religious import, sometimes led by the Señor Cura after Mass, accompanied by a doleful hymn on the Passion, sung antiphonally. Its name has wandered far from the original. The Contrapás de San Genis, for instance, is for six couples in a straight line, with a leader at each end. The influence of the antique Chain is strong in Catalonia and has resulted in several types of Farandole.

✣ DANCES BASED ON RITUAL ✣

An outline of the great wealth of ritual dances still practised in Spain is given later. But there remains another category —dances now recreational but with a ritual foundation. In these Catalonia is peculiarly rich. Some still contain pieces of nature magic, as fossils are embedded in rock. At Castelltersol the Ball del Ciri, Candle dance, is performed in church by the three outgoing churchwardens. Each man carries a *morratxa* (a glass jar filled with perfume) in one hand, a large candle in the other. The three new wardens receive these objects for the dance, after which they go to the porch and throw the *morratxas* on to its roof to break and allow the perfumed water to trickle down upon the spectators. There can be no doubt that this is rain magic —carried on by the Church authorities. Now follows La Dança. The villagers watch five couples issue from the church into the hot sunshine of the village square, the girls wearing white Pyrenean *capulets*, only to whisk them off and display lovely white lace mantillas—worn flat on the head, without the comb, in the Pyrenean manner. They revolve, the girls moving inwards, the men outwards in the form of curved spokes of a wheel.

Again, at Manlléu a man offers a girl a *morratxa* during the dance, which she immediately breaks. He brings her several more with the same result, though she accepts one at last.

At San Estéve de Sasrovires the Ball de les Crespelles (cakes) is performed at Easter. The men provide as many circular cakes with a hole in the middle as they can afford, which, during the dance, they hang upon the girls' arms. These cakes have a Spring-magical meaning in many Mediterranean countries; an egg—the perfect emblem of life—is embedded in the dough and cooked with it.

In the Vallés—a great valley not far from Barcelona—we find something falling almost into the category of the European folk play. Characters of the usual type are or were seen: the man in woman's clothes, the Ugly ones, the Pretty ones, the Old Couple, the Brides, Devils with fertilising whips, the age-old plough. Yet the dance is of so elaborate a form that the anthropological importance of these characters is apt to be overlooked. Eight to thirty-two couples may take part, Bride and Groom leading. Intricate and very beautiful figures are danced in different wheel-like patterns, with interludes of stepping in two rows —interludes called by misleading names such as Schottisch, Catxuxa and Jota, none of which they are. This is the Dance of the Gypsies—which again it is not, no gypsies being admitted.

ᵐᵝ *VALENCIA* ᶳᵚᵃ

Catalan traditions, meeting those of the South, make Valencian folk dance a particularly fascinating study. Valencia has its Jotas also. The most popular of these is the Jota Valenciana or Jota del Carrer (of the street), very different from the Aragonese type. Here the man leads his partner into the street, clears a space by spreading his striped blanket on the ground, the couple then dancing up to and away from it. Here is beautiful dancing, showing Andalusian influence yet free of Andalusian statuesque rigidity, free too of the tumult of pistol-like clapping and the incredible noise of *taconeado* (heel work). Something of the Catalan delicacy softens the style, and as (although guitars and voice take a part) the actual dancing is accompanied by the *dulzaïna* and *tabalet*, an almost Pyrenean flavour is given. The exquisite costumes of the Valencian Huerta add to a softened and lovely dance picture.

Apart from the Jota Valenciana we find the Arenilla, a Ball Rodó (Round) and a Ball Plá which are certainly of Catalan origin—as is the Valencian dialect. The Bolero Plá is a perfect example of an Eastern and Southern mixture, even to the two words of its name, while in the Copéo the South gains and introduces heel-tapping. Variants of the Fandango and Folías are also found.

❧ RITUAL DANCES OF SPAIN ❧

The amazing riches of ritual dances are here treated by types, covering the country as a whole, rather than by regions.

Bonfires belong alike to carnival and to midsummer. In the Eastern Pyrenees the Ball de les Faites (torches) is seen at both solstices. Men cut up tree trunks, set them alight, and in spite of their weight and the flames licking out at either end, dance with them on their shoulders through the villages. In Valencia city and district we see the famous *fallas* (bonfires), when life-sized, beautifully dressed figures are set alight and dancing goes on all through the night of March 19th—St. Joseph's Day. On Midsummer Eve the Pyrenean foothills are ablaze with fires, and fiesta continues all night long.

Plate 2
Valencia:
El U y el Dos

Sword and Stick Dances. These types of men's ritual dances
are found everywhere. Good Stick dancers are to be seen
round Soria, Castile; in Catalonia also, where at San Matéu
de Bajés the Ball de Cascabels (Bell dance) shows every
man with bells on his legs, a stick in his hand, and their
Chief Devil with a whip, cracking out orders to his men.
At Huesca, Aragon, they carry a stick in one hand, a sword
in the other; at Sena near by, the Sword dance merges into
a 'tower' and a play. A few villages on the southern Portu-
guese frontier, and other places, have ancient Sword dances.

Maypoles, Giants, Moriscas. Maypole dances are well
known, especially in Catalonia. The pole is often carried
about, the dancers each holding the end of a ribbon, form-
ing a lovely pattern and reciting topical verses. Giants are
very popular in Spain and often appear in pairs, Black and
White, huge figures up to eighteen feet in height, dancing
Quadrilles and looking down upon their accompanying
Dwarfs with huge comic heads.

Moriscas came into being as the Moors were driven south-
wards, and are so popular that their conquerors have never
ceased to fight them and dance with them all over Spain.
They begin under the very peaks of the Pyrenees in the
Mourisma of Ainsa, Aragon, 'Moors' and Christians shout-
ing bravado in the true spirit of the folk play. The most
gorgeous Moriscas are found in the Alcoy region south of
Valencia, where town fortifications become stage and back-
cloth, where 'Moors' ride into battle on disreputable mules
and wonderful companies of medieval Christians rush to
meet them.

Valencia, not so long ago, owned a folk ballet of great
richness, the Ball de Torrent, with a Viceroy and Vicereine,
the Fool, the Dragon and all the usual ritual characters.

The Seises. Dancing is by no means banished from religion
in Spain today, as is testified by the famous Seises of Seville.
These are boys dressed in the costume of the Philip II
period who, issuing from little golden doors, one on either

13

side the High Altar in Seville Cathedral, dance, castanets in hand, before the High Altar itself. This is always quoted as the last example of dancing in church, but there are many others.

One other strange Spring ebullition of a ritual character is the Carxofra (artichoke), or sometimes the Magrana (pomegranate)—both emblems of fertility—performed in Valencia. An enormous artichoke hangs from the roof or from a Maypole; flowers are distributed to the dancers after they have plaited the pole.

This summary gives but the merest outline of these survivals, beautiful, disconcerting, and of deepest anthropological as well as choreographical value, but it may at least serve to correct the persistent assertion that Andalusia is the only home of Spanish traditional dance.

⁂ MUSIC ⁂

North of the Ebro a Pyrenean type of music, song and dance prevails—south of that great river we touch the wonderful Catalan-Valencian and Southern mixture.

The bagpipe is still found in the Balearic Isles, Aragon, and, as we have seen, in Galicia.* Pipe and little drum are used in varying forms along the whole line of the Pyrenees. The pipe takes many names, *flaviol, dulzaïna, caramella* and, amongst the Spanish-Basques, *txistu.*

Catalonia possesses its Cobla band, used especially for Sardanas, in which the tiny flaviol and drum joins the strident prima and tenor with other instruments. Drums of all sizes are popular, from the midget slung on the left arm of the flaviol-player to the huge bombo, which stands as high as a man's waist. Panderos are square drums. Large shells employed in place of castanets in Rosas Bay recall a classic example of antiquity on the very spot of a Grecian trading post.

* See *Dances of Spain*, vol. 1, in this series.

Dance-songs are less general here than in Western regions, although the folk songs of Catalonia are numberless, simple and lovely.

Valencia has managed to amalgamate North and South even in her Jotas. A voice, accompanied by guitars, will sing the Copla, guitars will play the interlude, the local *du'zaïna* and *tabalet* (drum) will accompany the dance. Lovely folk songs exist, huerta and mountain types meeting Southern influence on the Murcian borders.

Aragon possesses Pyrenean pipe and drum, bagpipe and that strange wooden drum like an elongated box yet strung, its six strings beaten with a drum-stick. In the mountains of Jaca, where St. Orosia met her legendary death, her ritual dancers call it *salterio* or *chicotén*; it is played together with a small pipe by the same musician. The Basques across the mountains think it is their unique possession—the *ttun-ttun*—but in reality it is known in Béarn, Bigorre and Aragon as well as the Pays Basque.

Along the Ebro we have guitars, a Rondalla numbering up to twenty of them, the forced Jota voice and a strong Southern influence. Yet Aragon possesses simple and lovely folk songs modestly retired behind the Jota exhibitionism.

✤ COSTUME ✤

Aragon wears sober colours, the women's country dress showing striped aprons, voluminous petticoats and somewhat short skirts; the men wear short black velveteen breeches showing the puffy white pants at the knee. Rope-soled *alpargatas* with ties up the legs are worn by both sexes everywhere.

Wonderful medieval costumes are still worn in the Anso and Hecho valleys of Alto Aragón. The women's white, full sleeves form large, water-pleated puffs, while the forearm is covered with over-sleeves of velvet. Silk aprons hang from below the armpits, the chemise has an upstanding frill round the neck. Thus the silhouette is Renaissance. Here the men wear the primitive *abarca* or sandal strapped to the leg—said to be of Iberian origin. Plate 3 shows a couple from near Saragossa, the woman in silk or woollen shawl, cotton skirt and silk apron. Her kerchief is on the back of the head. The man wears the split-up breeches of black velveteen.

Catalonia. Plate 4 shows the dress of the towns and plains: shot-silk skirt, black satin bodice edged with lace, black mittens and lace shawl. The hair net, worn by men also, is a legacy from the fashion of Goya's time. The man's tight suit is of cloth.

Valencia (Plates 1 and 2) is devoted to lovely pastel shades, pale-flowered patterns, elaborate lace and flowered cottons. Even the men wear pale satins, as though a Neapolitan influence had crossed the sea. A knitted skull-cap with enormous tassels and satin slippers make an elegant town costume.

Down the coast and into Murcia starched and pleated white breeches look like skirts; a kerchief tied round the head or a red barretina sets off their dress. The women's gold, silver or copper combs and their 'earphones' of hair with silver pins follow a long tradition, dating in modified form from the Dama de Elche of Iberian ancestry.

OCCASIONS WHEN DANCING MAY BE SEEN

January 2nd — Malda (Catalonia). Men's sash dance outside the church.

January 17th — Caldas de Montbuy (Catalonia). Entrada de Ball, ceremonial dance.

February 14th — Mollet (Barcelona). Competitions for Gitanes, the Gypsy dance.

Carnival — Customs and dancing everywhere, especially on the Sunday, Monday and Tuesday before Lent.

March 19th, *St. Joseph's Day* — Valencia city and district. Fallas (bonfires) and dancing at night.

April 20th–30th — Alcoy (Alicante). Battle-drama of Moors and Christians.

Easter, Whitsuntide *and Ascension Day* — Maypole, Gitanes, Giants, Dwarfs and other manifestations everywhere. Bulls.

Corpus Christi — Ecclesiastical processions everywhere, often embracing folk elements.

June 23rd, Mid- *summer Eve* — Bonfires and dancing everywhere.

June 25th — Santa Orosia fiesta at Jaca (Aragon). Pilgrims, Stick dancers.

August 4th	Andorra la Vella. Patronal festival. Dances for three days.
August 9th–11th	Huesca (Aragon), Stick dances, Hobby Horses.
August 15th, Feast of the Assumption	Fiesta everywhere.
October 12th	Saragossa and district (Aragon). The great festival of Nuestra Señora del Pilar. Jotas all night. Bulls.

A Church Calendar is needed in Spain. Every Saint's Day is celebrated somewhere, every village has its own Patronal Saint with fiesta on that day.

⁓ [Spain, like many other countries, has emerged from the war period with her ancient practices in a state of flux. Groups with social-political leaders seem to have annexed the dances of the countryfolk, who see their inheritance interpreted by others. It is difficult now to find true traditional dancers and the utmost caution is necessary from the traditionist's point of view as regards competitions and displays of dancing.—*The Editor.*]

THE DANCES

TECHNICAL EDITORS
MURIEL WEBSTER AND KATHLEEN P. TUCK

꧁꧂

ABBREVIATIONS
USED IN DESCRIPTION OF STEPS AND DANCES

r—right⎱ referring to   R—right⎱ describing turns or
l—left ⎰ hand, foot, etc.   L—left ⎰ ground pattern
C—clockwise   C-C—counter-clockwise

For descriptions of foot positions and explanations of any ballet terms the following books are suggested for reference:

A Primer of Classical Ballet (Cecchetti method). Cyril Beaumont.

First Steps (R.A.D.). Ruth French and Felix Demery.

The Ballet Lover's Pocket Book. Kay Ambrose.

Reference books for description of figures:

The Scottish Country Dance Society's Publications. Many volumes, from Thornhill, Cairnmuir Road, Edinburgh 12.

The English Folk Dance and Song Society's Publications. Cecil Sharp House, 2 Regent's Park Road, London, N.W.1.

The Country Dance Book i–vi. Cecil J. Sharp. Novello & Co., London.

POISE OF BODY, ARM GESTURES AND BASIC STEPS

These will be described under regional headings, as there is much variation in types of dancing in the parts of Spain under discussion.

CATALONIA

The general poise of the body is upright with a slight backward lean from the waist. Men hold their arms loosely to the side, at times swinging them gently. In some dances,

e.g. Contrapás de Xinxina, the arms are raised to shoulder level, one bent across the chest, the other extended sideways. The position is reversed with a semi-circular sweep, hands still at shoulder level; the hands and wrists are flicked upward to mark the rhythm, the middle finger pointing down. The women occasionally use this arm movement, but they usually hold their skirts delicately between thumb and first finger, arms curved forward.

In the Sardana figure hands are joined, arms at shoulder level, elbows bent so that the hands are above the head. In the Entrada the men hold r hands forward, palms up, while the women place l hands lightly on partners' r-hands, only the fingers touching.

Skipping. Raise free foot behind the knee of supporting leg and place it exactly in front of the supporting foot. (Knee pointing forward, ankle extended.) In the Sardana figure the free foot is raised behind the knee of the other leg, the feet moving sideways so that dancers may face the centre of the circle with hands grasped as described above.

Ball Plá. A gliding Pas de Basque with the accent on the second beat.

Little Walk (women only). 3/4 time. A triple run or walk, rising high on balls of feet on beats 2 and 3, body bending slightly to R or L on every third step.

Jetés, Polka steps, Entrechats, Cabrioles, Ronds-de-jambes and Ballonnés are frequently used also.

VALENCIA

The poise is upright with a slight backward lean from the waist, arms and shoulders generally held in open line—the same shoulder and leg forward. The arms are never fully stretched or bent but curved, so no angle is shown at the elbow. They move in downward circles from above the head—outward until the elbow is at shoulder level, then the forearm descends with the wrist leading. The hand close to the body goes up the middle, past the face, to above the head. Each arm in turn takes three beats to move slowly above head, and three more to move quickly from shoulder round and up again. Thus there is always one arm above the head. The body moves from the waist to R when the l arm is above the l leg, and to L when the r arm is above the r leg. Arm and leg always move together. The head should be held well back, looking over the free shoulder as the arm moves down.

A detailed description of simple Valencian steps is given in El U y el Dos.

Valencian use of Castanets. The easiest rhythm is called 'Aria, Aria, Pita'—a mnemonic formula, thus:

Ari-á, Ari-á, Pi-tá
and 1 and 2 and 3

i.e. three beats (one bar) for the whole rhythm. On each 'Ari-á' roll four fingers of the right hand beginning with the little finger, left hand beating the á of 'Ari-á', making five sounds in all. On 'Pi-tá' the right hand sounds Pi, the left hand sounds tá, two sounds in all.

ARAGON

The body leans back from the waist, hips forward and head upright. Knees are somewhat bent throughout. Arms are raised forward at shoulder level, slightly curved with elbows out and wrists and hands loose for playing of castanets. A full description of arm movements, and of some of the many steps, is given in the notation of the Jota, page 33.

There are two kinds of Jota, a slow one, and the quick Dancing Jota. The steps may be divided into two types: those danced during the Estribillo (B and C music), and those danced during the verse or Copla (A and D music). The Estribillo or chorus appears in both types, slow when sung, quick when danced. Steps for the Estribillo are: Pas de Basque, Snatch steps backwards, and a variety of gliding, high-springing and high-kicking steps. All of these are performed while partners face each other and move C in one complete circle back to places; the man tries to encircle the girl with his arms at every 3rd bar; she escapes by pivoting out of his grasp. Steps for the verse or Copla are:—

Side-stamp step
Step and hop on r foot, turning l shoulder towards partner [*beats 1 and 2*]; place l heel in front of r foot (changing weight) and bending forward from the waist with backs

of wrists touching in front, arms curved [*beat 3*]; step and hop on r foot, leaning back and opening arms outward and backward [*beats 1, 2*]; place l toe behind r toe (changing weight) [*beat 3*]; step and hop on r foot, bending forwards, backs of wrists touching [*beats 1, 2*]; place whole of l foot in front of r foot (changing weight) [*beat 3*]; turn sharply to L on ball of l foot, turning r shoulder towards partner [*beat 1*]; stamp twice on r foot, leaning back with arms raised above head [*beats 2, 3*].

Repeat the whole step, beginning on l foot. Partners look at one another throughout.

Turning step

Jump on both feet, turning a quarter to L [*beats 1, 2*]; hop on l foot, r foot behind the knee, turning quarter to R [*beat 3*]; 3 steps, r l r, turning a whole turn and moving to the R [*beats 1, 2, 3*].

Repeat the whole step hopping on r foot and moving and turning to L. Partners look at one another as they move diagonally in opposite directions.

Aragonese use of castanets. The loops are slipped over middle finger of each hand. Click is made by second and third finger together. The rhythm is:

♩ ♪ ♪ ♩

Play: both hands—beat 1; r hand—beat 2; l hand—'and'; r hand—beat 3.

CONTRAPÁS DE XINXINA

Region   Pallars, Catalonia.

Character   Gay and light, with dignified bearing.

Formation   Open ring or semicircle of six to twenty couples. Later a circle.

Dance   The men's arm movement, which continues throughout, is described on page 20. Women hold skirts with both hands (see Plate 4).

ENTRADA. Couples enter C-C, men on inside of ring. Woman's l hand rests lightly on man's r hand, which is held forward at waist level, palm facing up. When all are in semicircle the 1st man nods to the other men, who lead partners C-C (three-quarter turn) to places, the women *on left of men* in a single ring. All face inward except 1st couple, who face C-C. (○ = woman, □ = man.)

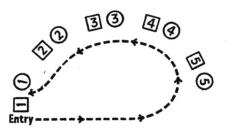

	MUSIC
1a 1st man skips C-C across front and round semicircle, two skips to each bar, for 11 bars. On bar 12 he jumps R about to face his partner. He starts with arms held to L side and moves them from L to R for 12 skips, flick-	Bars A 1–6 rep't'd

ing his wrists on every skip, then from R to L, finishing with arms to L.

1b CHORUS. Man dances backward away from his partner, 5 skips, beginning with r foot and stepping forward on l foot for 6th skip. Partners bow to one another on 5th skip, man's arms move from L to R. He repeats this, dancing forward to partner for 5 skips and backward on the 6th. Arms move from R to L. Repeat the whole movement backwards and forwards.	B 7–18
Man jumps R about, leaving his arms to L.	19
1c Repeat 1a, 1st woman following her partner in the semicircle, jumping feet together without a turn on last step.	A 1–6 rep't'd
1d Repeat 1b, the woman always skipping forward and backward while the man does the opposite. She does not turn at the end but jumps feet together.	B 7–19
The above movements are repeated, a new couple joining in each time, dancing the Chorus facing partner. The last time, couples form a closed ring during A music and dance the Chorus in this formation, all jumping to face centre, with hands joined, on last bar.	AAB re-peated
2a SARDANA. All dance 10 skips C, beginning with l foot, facing centre of circle during the skips. Close feet together, hold for one beat. Repeat C-C, beginning with r foot.	A 1–6 1–6
2b With hands still joined, all take 6 small steps forward on flat of feet, bringing arms downward and forward upward to shoulder level; 6 long steps backward to form as wide a circle as possible.	B 7–9 10–12

CONTRAPÁS DE XINXINA

Noted by Lucile Armstrong
Arranged by Arnold Foster

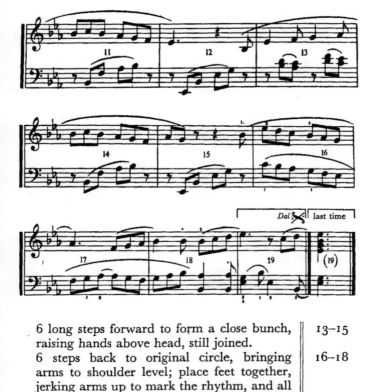

6 long steps forward to form a close bunch, raising hands above head, still joined.	13–15
6 steps back to original circle, bringing arms to shoulder level; place feet together, jerking arms up to mark the rhythm, and all bend forward, stretching arms forward.	16–18
	19
Exeunt. Each leads off the woman on his R, not his own partner.	

N.B.—In all skipping steps the free foot must be raised to knee height—knee facing straight forward and ankle extended.

Figure 2a is called 'Sardana' but is not the dance of that name.

EL U Y EL DOS (*The One and the Two*)

ᴴᴴᴴᴴᴴᴴᴴᴴ

Region   Valencia city and district.

Chara:ter Light supple movements; danced in the streets
             to the accompaniment of guitar and castanets.

Formation Individual couples walk on to the dance space,
             the man carrying his blanket over his left shoul-
             der. He lays the blanket on the ground, and the
             couple face one another.

Dance	MUSIC
1 Partners stand with l feet in front (3rd posi-	*Bars*
tion); r hand on hip and l hand to side. The	
step marks a V formation on the ground.	**A**
Step forward on l foot, turning shoulders to	1
R and raising both arms curved above head,	(beat 1)
l shoulder directly above l foot; close r foot	(beat 2)
behind on toe, clicking castanets against one	
another above head; step back on r foot,	(beat 3)
clicking castanets with hands apart. Place	2
l toe to r toe (5th position), moving l arm	(beat 1)
down, elbow out; kick l foot diagonally for-	(beat 2)
ward to waist level with knee bent, l arm	
circling down past knee and up close to body;	
step l foot behind r foot, l arm completing	(beat 3)
the circle to position above head. (This step	
is similar to the Paso de Entrada in Seguidillas	
Sevillanas: see *Dances of Spain*, vol. 1.)	
Castanets: During these two bars play 'Ariá,	
Ariá, Pitá' twice (see page 22).	

Plate 3
Aragon: Jota

EL U Y EL DOS

Noted by Lucile Armstrong
Arranged by Arnold Foster

Repeat above step on r foot without clicking castanets [*beat 2*], r arm describing circle.	3–4
Repeat above step on l and r foot alternately: seven and a half times in all.	5–15
Place feet together, turning to face blanket, partners side by side [*beats 1 and 2*].	16

2 Raise r foot in front of l knee, leaning over r shoulder to look at r foot; arms raised forward with backs of wrists touching [*beat 3*].   **B**

Place r foot behind l knee [*beat 1*]; step back on r foot [*beat 2*]; step back on l foot [*beat 3*].   17

Step forward on r foot [*beat 1*].   18

This phrase of 5 beats is repeated 4 times with alternate feet, the arms swinging easily forward, outward and backward with the hands at waist level. Finish facing partner, with feet together.   18–24

The castanets click the 'Ariá' rhythm throughout, once to each musical beat, thus giving an even roll without the marked 'Pitá'.

3 Repeat 1, dancing it 4 times in all, beginning with l foot; click castanets on 3rd beat of bar 32.   **C**
                                                                            25–32

Point l foot forward; bring r arm above the head and well back, l arm below the shoulder across chest. Click castanets on last chord and jerk the head back, looking at partner. Hold.   33

JOTA

ᕼᕼᕼᕼᕼᕼᕼ

Region   Aragon.

Character   Light, cat-like steps on flexed knees to castanet
accompaniment. The man shows off his agility
to the woman, who follows his steps.

Formation   For any number of couples.

Dance	MUSIC *Bars*
During the two-bar introduction partners stand facing one another. Throughout the dance, unless otherwise stated, the upper arms are held at shoulder level, with elbow bent outwards, back of wrists forwards with hands hanging loosely to play castanets.	
1*a* OPENING STEP. This step is always danced first, the others at will.	A
Hop on l foot, pointing r toe to l toe, almost touching [*beats 1 and 2*]. Hop on l foot, r foot describing a semicircle in the air, knee bent close to l knee, lower leg held sideways at knee-level [*beat 3*]. (See Plate 3.)	1
Step on r foot behind l foot [*beat 1*]; step sideways on l foot [*beat 2*]; step on r foot in front of l foot [*beat 3*]. (The movements of this bar constitute a Pas de Bourrée.)	2
Repeat above, hopping on r foot and travelling to L.	3–4
Repeat the whole step, first on l then on r foot.	5–8

Arranged by Arnold Foster

1*b* Hop on l foot, pointing r toe forward as in first step; hop on l foot, circling r foot sideways as in first step. | 9

Hop on l foot, touching r toe to l heel [*beats 1 and 2*]; hop on l foot, circling r foot sideways and forward [*beat 3*]. | 10

Repeat the movement as in bar 9. | 11

1 Pas de Bourrée travelling to L. | 12

Repeat above step, hopping on r foot and travelling to R. | 13–16

Hop on l foot forward as before [*beats 1 and 2*]; hop on l foot, circling r foot as before [*beat 3*]. | 17

Link between steps 1 and 2: Point r toe forward [*beats 1 and 2*]; transfer weight on to r foot [*beat 3*]. | B 18

2 SIDE-STEP

Step sideways on l foot [*beat 1*]; hop on l foot, keeping r leg extended sideways [*beat 2*]; close r foot towards l foot, changing weight [*beat 3*]. | 19

Repeat above movement twice, but on last beat of bar 21 spring on r foot, pointing l foot forward. | 20–21

3 springs, alternately pointing r l r feet forward. | 22

Repeat 3 Side-steps on r foot, moving to R, and finish with spring on l foot, pointing r foot forward. | 23–25

3 springs, alternately pointing l r l feet forward. | 18

Repeat 3 Side-steps on l foot. | 19–21

Hop on l foot, pointing l foot sideways [*beat 1*]; 5 hops on l foot, raising r knee and swinging r foot from the knee to L R L R L [*beats 2 3, 1 2 3*]. | 22–23

Spring on r foot and repeat 5 hops on r foot, swinging l foot to R L R L R. | 24–25

Arm movement. During Side-steps to L the hips are jerked to L with a slight bend of body to R, so that l arm is raised to head level and r arm lower. (Arms still curved.) The movement of body and arms is reversed when travelling to R.

3 FLICK STEP. The ground pattern of this step is a V. | C

Step on l foot to change weight. | 26

Step diagonally forward to L on r foot, raising l leg to waist level [*beat 1*]; hop on r foot, flicking skirt with toe of raised l foot [*beat 2*]; step diagonally forward on l foot [*beat 3*]. | 27

Repeat this step, still travelling diagonally to L. During these two bars the l arm is held, slightly curved, along the line of l leg, the r arm curved slightly above head level. | 28

3 Step hops travelling back to place, hopping on r l r feet and circling the free leg backwards, with knee straight, on each Step hop. Arms change to opposite position. | 29–30

Repeat 2 Flick steps diagonally forward to R on l foot. | 31–32

3 Step hops back to place on l r l feet. | 33, 26
2 Flick steps diagonally forward to L on r foot. | 27–28
3 Step hops back to place on r l r feet. | 29–30
4 Pas de Basque on spot on l r l r feet. | 31–34

4 KNEELING STEP | D

Step on l foot turning to L so that r knee touches ground. Partners look at one another, l arm curved above shoulder level, r arm raised sideways [*beat 1*]; rise swiftly on | 35

37

both feet, beginning to turn to R [*beats 2 and 3*].

Repeat kneeling step to R and rise on both feet.	36
Push off with r foot, beginning to turn to L [*beat 1*]; turn on ball of l foot [*beat 2*]; place r foot sideways to face partner [*beat 3*]. When turning always raise free foot to back of the knee of supporting leg.	37
Hop on l foot placing r toe sideways on ground, knee turned in and arms as in kneeling step [*beat 1*]; hold position [*beat 2*]; hop on l foot, placing r heel on ground, knee turned out [*beat 3*].	38
3 hops on l foot, repeating toe-heel-toe movement on each beat. Hop on l foot, placing r toe to l toe [*beat 1*]; whip r foot in circling action (Rond-de-jambe) twice, hopping on l foot on 3rd beat and turning half-turn to R.	39 40
3 steps turning to R, moving slightly leftward on r l r feet to face partner.	41
Repeat the toe-heel movements as in bars 38 and 39, but hopping on r foot.	42–43
Repeat the Rond-de-jambe and 3 turning steps to L on l r l feet.	44–45
Change weight in place r l. Man springs to kneeling position on r knee while woman places one foot on his knee and leans away from him. Beat castanets together on last beat.	46
Both dancers have one arm curved above the head, the other across the chest. Click castanets on final chord. Hold.	47

Plate 4
Catalonia: Contrapás de Xinxina

BIBLIOGRAPHY

ALFORD, VIOLET.—'The Valencian Cross-roads.' In *The Musical Quarterly*, New York, July, 1937.
—— 'Some Notes on the Pyrenean Stringed Drum.' In *Revue Internationale des Etudes Basques*, vol. xxvi, July, 1933.
—— 'Santa Orosia, a Thaumaturgic Saint.' In *Antiquity*, September, 1934.
—— 'The Dance of the Gypsies in Catalonia.' In *Journal of the English Folk Dance and Song Society*, vol. i, No. 3, 1934.
AMADES, JOAN.—*El Ball de les Gitanes*. Barcelona, 1925. (The Dance of the Gypsies.)
ARCO, RICARDO DEL.—*Costumbres y Trajes en los Pirineos*. Saragossa, 1930. (Customs and costume in the Pyrenees.)
—— *Aragón*. Huesca, 1931.
CAPMANY, AURELI.—*El Ball i la Dansa Popular a Catalunya*. Barcelona, 1948.
CARRERA Y CANDÍ (ed.).—*Folklore y Costumbres de España*, vol. ii. Barcelona, 1931.
LITRORY, DON J. R. DE.—*Diccionario de Musicos Valencianos*. Valencia, 1903.
MASPONS Y MASO.—*El Ball de les Gitanes en el Vallés*. Barcelona, 1907. (The Dance of the Gypsies in the Valleys.)
TORNER, E. M.—*Danzas Valencianas*. Barcelona, 1938.